For A.D.B. & co., love R.

Copyright © 1991 Ruth Gembicki Bragg
Published by Picture Book Studio, Saxonville, MA.
All rights reserved.
Printed in Hong Kong.
10 9 8 7 6 5 4 3 2 1

Library of Congress Cataloging in Publication Data
Bragg, Ruth.
Alphabet out loud / by Ruth Gembicki Bragg
Summary: Illustrations and poetic text depict a playful tour of the alphabet.
ISBN 0-88708-172-X : $14.95
1. English language—Alphabet—Juvenile literature.
[1. Alphabet.] I. Title.
PE1155.B65   1991
421'.1—dc20   91-14546

Ask your bookseller for these other Picture Book Studio books
by Ruth Gembicki Bragg:
Mrs. Muggle's Sparkle
The Birthday Bears

ALPHABET OUT LOUD

Ruth Gembicki Bragg

Picture Book Studio

A is for All of us
Agreeing to shout A,
All at the same time.
Get ready! Get set!
Here we go!
A!

OH OH! OOOPS! Shhh!
Because B is for a Big Bunch of Babbling Babies
who were about to take their naps.
Hush, you babies. Hush, be still.
Lie down, be quiet and close your eyes.
Ahhh. That's better.
We will try not to bother you again.

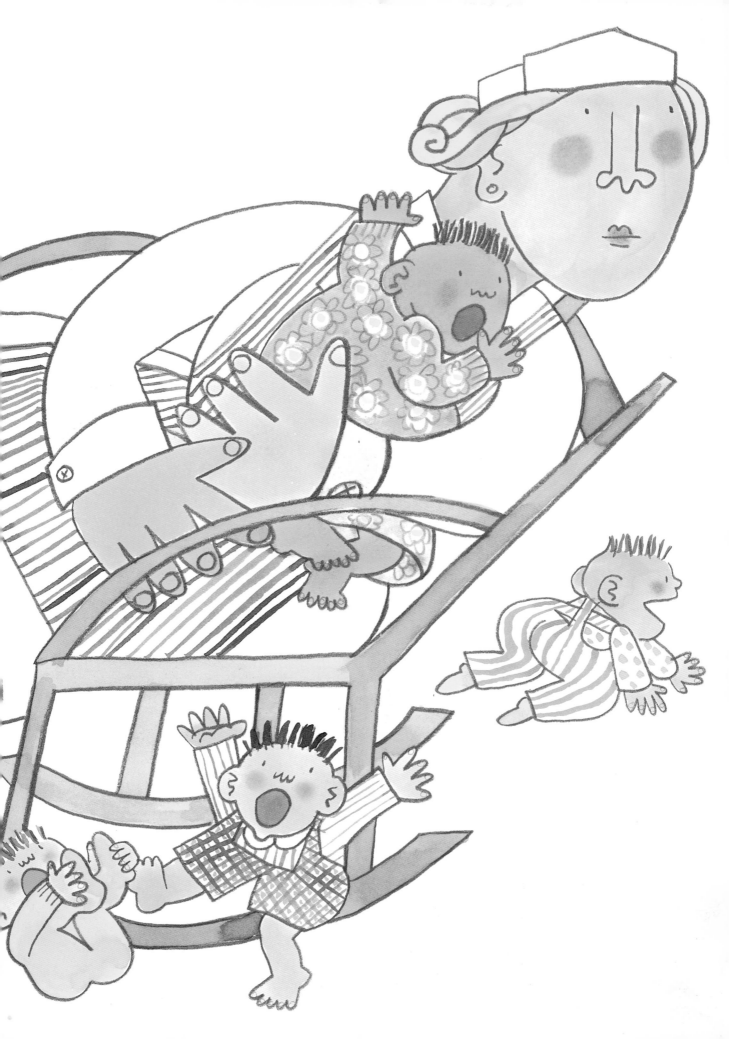

C is for a Crowd of Cats
busy practicing their caterwauling:
MRRROW!

Get down, you dog.
You are not a cat.

D is for Daddy's Home!

E and F are for Eating Fudge.
(To make Fudge to Eat:
melt 18 ounces of chocolate chips;
add 15 ounces of sweet condensed milk,
a pinch of salt, and 1½ teaspoons of vanilla.
Stir. Line a square pan with waxed paper.
Pour in the fudge. Put the pan into the
refrigerator for 2 hours.)
Oh, it is hard to wait that long!
Is it time to taste yet?

G and H are for Ghouly Ghosts Happily Howling.
HOOOO! Watch out!
We're the terrible Goggle-eyed,
Hairy-faced Hob-Goblin Gang!
GRRRR!

Hocus-pocus!
Harum-scarum!
Hurry-scurry!
Get out, Ghosts!
Harrumph!

I is Incredible.
I is for me, myself, I.
And I am incredible.
When you say I, I is you,
and you are incredible too!
To me, I am I and you are you.
But you are I to you,
and I am you to you.
Incredible!

J is for the Jibber Jabber Jackpot.
Congratulations.
You just won it with your jabber.

K is for Knowing that you Know
how to do some things pretty well.
What do you know? Will you teach me?

I know how to make a telephone. Do you?

L is for Learning.
Now that we know that, what shall we learn next?
We'll be the lalapaloozas of cleverness!
The Lord and Lady of bright ideas!

M and N are for Making enormous Noises.
I imagine that we make as much noise
as a million minnows. Maybe more.

O and P are for Opening Presents.
Pull off the paper! Pry off the top!
What did you get?
What do you think will be in mine?

Q and R are for Questions and for Riddles,
which are questions without real answers.
I'll tell you one if you tell me two:
What is the difference between a mailbox
and a garbage can? Give up?
Then I won't ask you to mail my letters for me.
Your turn now.

S is for Singing,
even if we don't know the words.
We can make those up as we go along.
This is our super sounding song–
La!La!La!La!La!
Shall we sing it again?
Yes! Louder this time.

T is for Thinking.
Clouds and stars help,
but with a little practice you can do it anywhere.
Watch carefully. See that? I'm thinking.
Do you think that what I'm thinking about
thinks about me too?

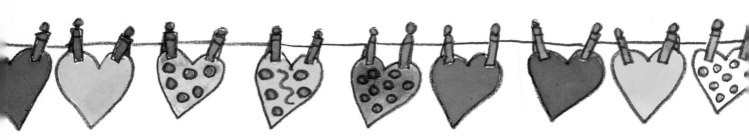

If U is for Us, then V is for Valentines, of course.

W is for Wishing.
With skies full of stars, we will always
have enough wishes in the world to go around.
W is also for having a whole head full of wondering,
like wondering which wish to wish for
and wondering if my wish will come true and when.
The hardest part of wishing is waiting.

X is what Grandma writes at the bottom of her letters.

Dear
Children,
I wish I
that I
could see
you soon
xxxooo
NoNNA

YAH AHH. AHH YAH.
Y is for Yawning.
If there were a World Championship
of Yawning, I would win it.
No one can yawn better than I can.
I dare you to try. YAHHH!
Hear that? I win again!
But watch out! Yawning is contagious.
Once I yawn, you have to yawn too.
YAHHHH.

ZZZZZ.
Drowsy babies snuggle into zippered sleepers.
Hear the good snoozers! ZZZZZ!
Take it easy! Babies! Please!
You will shake us silly
with your snorey noises.

But I can snore better
than these babies.
I can snore this long:
ZZZZZZZZZZZZZZ
with just one breath.
Now you try.